MODERN
MASTERS

Contemporary Architecture
from around the World

Steve
HUYTON

Schiffer Publishing Ltd.

4880 Lower Valley Road • Atglen, PA 19310

Other Schiffer Books by Steve Huyton:
Luxury Design for Living, ISBN 978-0-7643-5421-2
Limited Edition Watches: 150 Exclusive Modern Designs, ISBN 978-0-7643-5164-8

Other Schiffer Books on Related Subjects:
Contemporary Texas Architecture, E. Ashley Rooney, ISBN 978-0-7643-5238-6

Designed by Danielle D. Farmer
Cover design by Danielle D. Farmer
Cover photo by Victor Sajara
Back cover photos by Bates Masi + Architects (top), David Franck (middle left), Ali Bekman (middle right), David Ross and Barend Roberts (bottom)
Endsheets: Christian Richters (front), William MacCollum (back)

Type set in Benton Sans/Life

ISBN: 978-0-7643-5384-0
Printed in China

Published by Schiffer Publishing, Ltd.
4880 Lower Valley Road
Atglen, PA 19310
Phone: (610) 593-1777; Fax: (610) 593-2002
E-mail: Info@schifferbooks.com
Web: www.schifferbooks.com

For our complete selection of fine books on this and related subjects, please visit our website at www.schifferbooks.com. You may also write for a free catalog.

Schiffer Publishing's titles are available at special discounts for bulk purchases for sales promotions or premiums. Special editions, including personalized covers, corporate imprints, and excerpts, can be created in large quantities for special needs. For more information, contact the publisher.

We are always looking for people to write books on new and related subjects. If you have an idea for a book, please contact us at proposals@schifferbooks.com.

Contents

Contents

I became interested in architecture at a very young age, and until recently, I preferred historic buildings. Certainly in the UK there are many old properties with an enormous amount of charm, and their detailing displays a level of craftsmanship seldom found in today's world. In general, I found modern buildings to be generic and devoid of character. However, some of the modernist homes that twenty-first-century architects are designing are absolutely phenomenal. This collection of houses showcases the talents of eighteen forward-thinking international architects. Many of the buildings feature an abundance of glass, steel, and concrete and are presented on an epic scale, several times larger than the average family home—modernism writ large. While hand craftsmanship is not always front and center, they are unique examples of creativity and often exhibit innovative engineering feats of great beauty. I hope you are as dazzled by these magnificent homes as I am.

A-CERO

Madrid

A-cero, founded by architects Joaquin Torres and Rafael Llamazares, has designed private houses for clients around the world, including in Europe, UAE, Lebanon, Russia, Saudi Arabia, and the US. They draw inspiration from the work of Le Corbusier and Mies, as well as John Pawson and Spanish architects Ignacio Ramos and Jose Antonio Vicens.

A-CERO

Concrete House
Madrid

This architectural gem seems to be hidden between dark gray concrete walls and vegetated ramps that slope up toward the roof. Its 16,145 square feet (1,500 square meters) contain a lounge/dining room/kitchen, office, living room, and four bedrooms with full bathrooms. The rear of the house is completely open to the garden terraces and a large pool. Rooftop solar collectors supply the home's energy needs.

House in Madrid
Madrid

This home in the heart of Madrid was completed nearly twenty years ago and has stood the test of time. Travertine marble on the exterior continues inside as flooring, and a large marble cylinder organizes the first-floor living spaces. The upper floor houses the bedrooms and baths and the library, which is built along a glass walkway overlooking the main drawing room.

A-CERO

Los Lagos
Madrid

Built in Madrid's exclusive Pozuelo de Alarcón area, the 8,072-square-foot (1,750-square-meter) house has strong horizontal lines and stylized curves that appear to rise from the earth. Its facades are covered in texturized dark concrete that reinforces the geological association. The ground level houses the living areas, master bedroom, gym, and indoor pool. Upstairs is a painting studio with views over the landscape, and the basement holds a bar, game room, and theater. Throughout, large-format white ceramic floor tiles accentuate the flowing spaces.

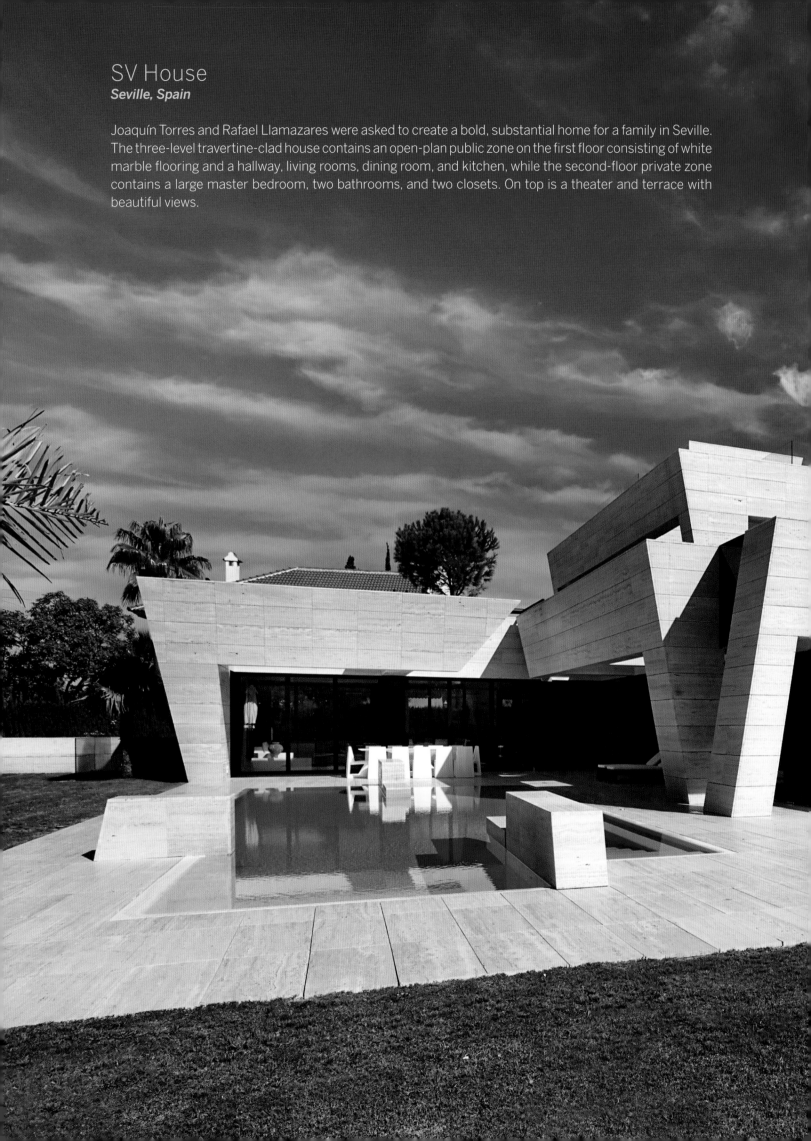

SV House
Seville, Spain

Joaquín Torres and Rafael Llamazares were asked to create a bold, substantial home for a family in Seville. The three-level travertine-clad house contains an open-plan public zone on the first floor consisting of white marble flooring and a hallway, living rooms, dining room, and kitchen, while the second-floor private zone contains a large master bedroom, two bathrooms, and two closets. On top is a theater and terrace with beautiful views.

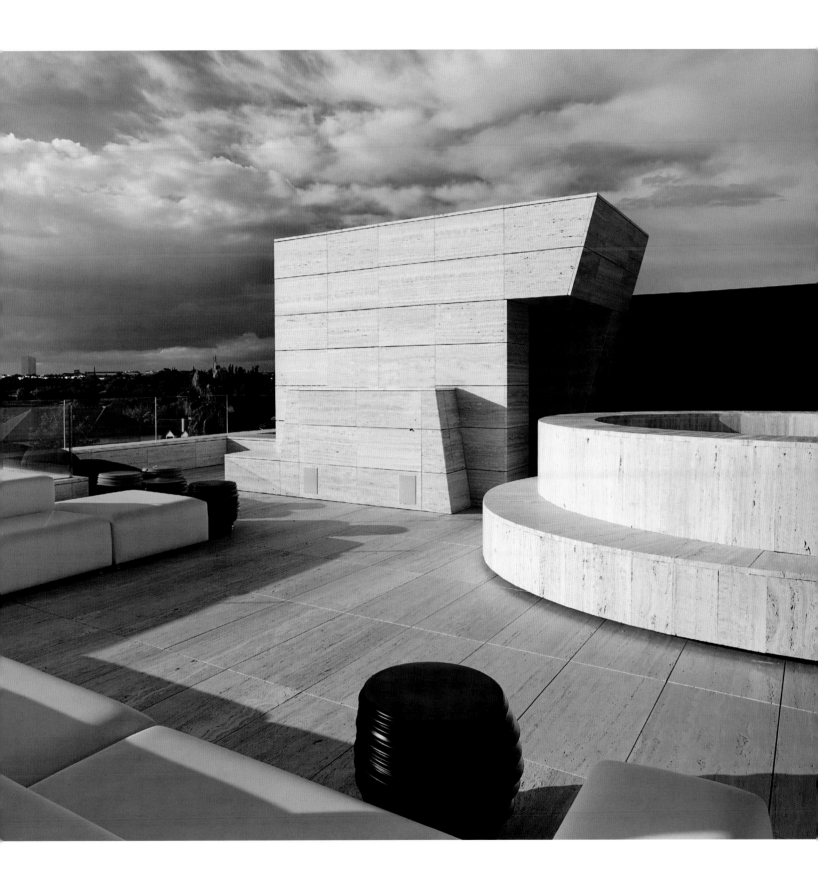

AR DESIGN STUDIO

Hampshire, England

Andy Ramus founded AR Design Studio more than fifteen years ago after working on large-scale projects in London for several years. Each commission, ranging from new builds to innovative additions, demonstrates that great richness can be achieved by creating an environmentally friendly building that focuses on the needs of the client and site.

Glass House
Hampshire, England

A frameless glass extension to the rear of a traditional house transformed gloomy servants' quarters into light and airy communal spaces. The architects cut vertical voids through the house to connect the cellar, ground, and first floors and redirect circulation to the new glass space housing the kitchen, living, and dining areas. The remodel and addition accentuate the contrast between light and dark, openness and seclusion. Timber ceramic tiling was chosen because it won't fade in the bright sunlight, absorbs the radiant floor heating, and runs seamlessly out to the cantilevered patio.

AR DESIGN STUDIO

Lighthouse 65
Hill Head, Fareham, England

Lighthouse 65 sits between two neighboring homes on the south coast of England with far-reaching views of the English Channel and Isle of Wight. Because the house is twenty-three feet (seven meters) below street level, the roof is used as a parking deck for three cars. A central, frameless glass access tower acts as a lighthouse; it's fitted with a barometer that triggers a green or red glow to indicate local weather conditions at night, warning passing yachtsmen of foul weather. The house, which cantilevers from a concrete core, is long and narrow so that all living spaces have a continuous view.

Richmond House
Richmond, England

A characterless four-bedroom, neo-Georgian house was transformed with a substantial addition that contains a new master bedroom, walk-in wardrobe, large living space, and state-of-the-art kitchen. The brick-clad side tower, connected to the house with a glass link that brings light into the building, contains a utility room on the ground floor and a master suite above. A single-story extension at the rear of the house made room for a large, open-plan kitchen, dining, and living space. It is covered in tessellated fiber-cement panels and opens seamlessly to the mature gardens with bi-folding doors.

Pilot's House
Hampshire, England

The Pilot's House is a grand mid-nineteenth-century villa in Winchester, Hampshire. The architects fastidiously restored the house to its former glory and added a contemporary wing containing a communal living area and indoor swimming pool. This extension is covered by a roof pitched to the east toward an old boundary wall and the rising sun, and clad in anthracite zinc to tie in with the house's slate tiles. The two roofs above the living space address the level changes and help to blur the boundary between old and new. The extension's glazed southern façade is shaded by an overhanging canopy and colonnade, in keeping with the historic house's grandeur.

ARTechnic
ARCHITECTS

Tokyo

Founded in 1994, ARTechnic Architects is the brainchild of industry veteran Kotaro Ide. The company has a small team of specialists including president Kotaro Ide, assistant architect Ruri Mitsuyasu, and metalwork designer Manami Kawamura.

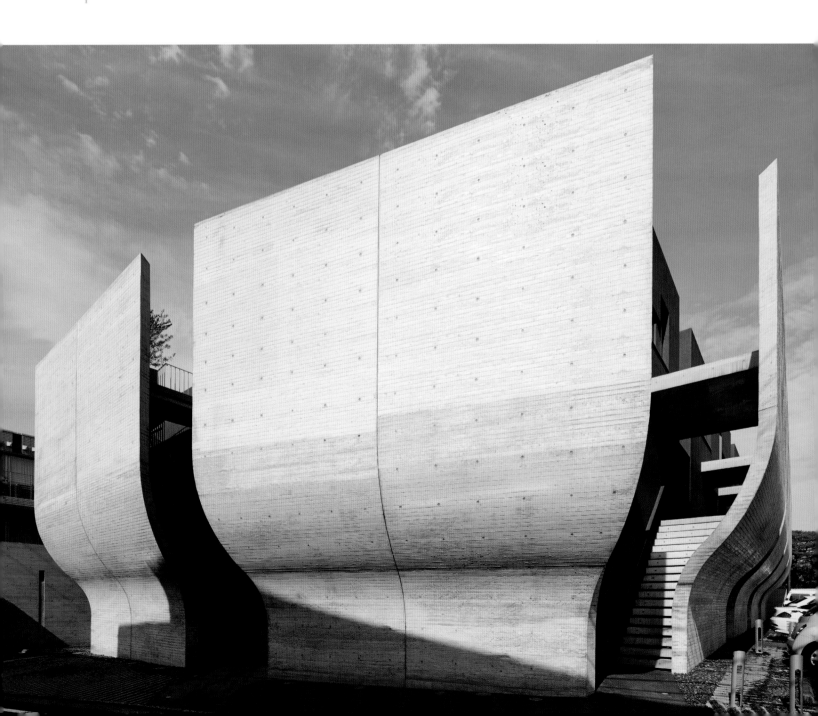

Breeze
Toyko

Breeze is a private getaway in the Tokyo suburb of Meguro and sits next to the former home of a notable twentieth-century prime minister. The architect describes Breeze as an "impassive signpost" with an "entrance that recalls a crevice to a secret rock cave." The sinuous concrete facade addresses the client's request for privacy from the busy street, while the 13,465-square-foot (1,251-square-meter) interior faces south, opening up "like a private beach" set against a "soaring rock face." The concrete is softened by the use of glass, wood, walnut plywood, aluminum, and steel.

Rosie
Tokyo

Land goes for a premium in the Tokyo suburb of Setagaya, and Rosie sits on an awkward, 13,465-square-foot (1,251-square-meter) strip of land running east-west. This meant that Kotaro Ide had to be very creative with the space. Only 1,625 square feet (151 square meters), the house has two parallel lines that form the main axis, while the street angle and west boundary form other axes. These angles are mediated with a gate-like front facade featuring a roof slab and side walls that face the street head-on. Outer walls are insulated concrete forms, and interior walls are plastered. The clever use of angles, glass, and timber align the house with the site and make the building appear larger than it is.

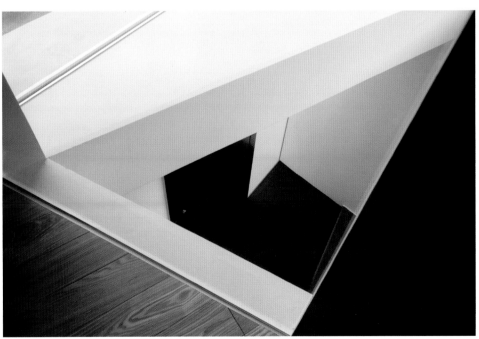

Shell
Nagano, Japan

Shell is located in the popular summer resort area of Karuizawa, Nagano, and appears to have come from outer space. Though it is nestled in nature, it is made to endure nature's ravages. Curling around a mature fir tree at the center of the site, the 3,541-square-foot (329-square-meter), J-shaped concrete structure consists of two different-size cylindrical masses, one containing a double-height living space. The lower half of the shell structure extends outside and supports a wooden terrace. This home's organic, wood-wrapped interior creates a harmonious living environment.

SRK
Tokyo

Although SRK, in the heart of Meguro, Tokyo, occupies a relatively small 2,523-square-foot (234-square-meter) site and measures just 1,894 square feet (176 square meters), it has been maximized to its full potential. A retaining wall becomes part of the architecture, a rising spiral that wraps around the building and edits the view of a close neighbor. The upper floor's large windows lend a feeling of dwelling among the trees. Solid walnut flooring helps to ground the house on its site.

ARTechnic ARCHITECTS

Assemblage STUDIO

Las Vegas

AssemblageSTUDIO is a progressive architectural practice established by Eric Strain in 1997. As its name suggests, the firm prefers to take a collaborative approach to projects, working with clients in a spirit of mutual respect to develop appropriate ways to live and work in a desert environment.

Copper HAUS
Las Vegas

Copper, rammed earth, solid timber, and an abundance of glass help Copper HAUS blend into its site, which slopes steeply from front to back. The upper level is supported on rammed earth walls, grounding the design. The multi-level design allows each floor to receive abundant natural light, and movement through the house reveals vast panoramas and framed views of intimate courtyards. The floor plan culminates in a roof deck offering unrestricted views of Bear's Best golf course at the base of the Red Rock Mountains and the distant Las Vegas Strip.

AssemblageSTUDIO

House in 2 Parts
Las Vegas

Situated in the idyllic foothills of the Red Rock Mountains in the southwestern part of Las Vegas, House in 2 Parts is divided into two parts—the main living area for the owners and the guest quarters. The volumes are separated by a cleverly designed bridge, which also doubles as an outdoor living area.

House of Light and Water
Las Vegas

House of Light and Water is a tranquil family home in a hidden oasis in Fletcher Canyon. The H-shaped footprint consists of a one-story entertaining volume clad in black steel and containing two living areas and a kitchen. The two-story bedroom wing is wrapped in CMU plaster and weathered wood. Linking the two areas are the entry and dining room. The house's cleverly conceived forms echo the surrounding canyon landscape and create a play of light and shadow.

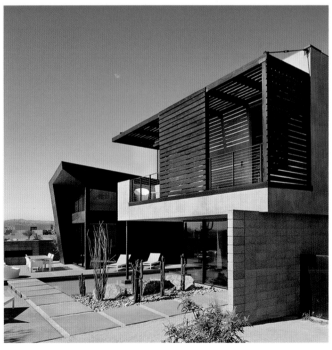

J2 Residence
Las Vegas

The J2 residence is in Summerlin, along the western edge of Las Vegas at the base of Red Rock. The clients asked for a harmonious living environment that effortlessly blends with the outdoors. They also wanted to maximize views of the adjacent golf course and foothills. Kyocera multi-crystal photovoltaic modules on the wing canopy generate forty percent of the house's electrical load.

BATES MASI+ ARCHITECTS

Sagaponack, New York

Bates Masi + Architects, owned by Harry Bates and Paul Masi, is an architectural practice with deep roots in New York City and the East End of Long Island dating back more than fifty years. In addition to designing a range of exquisite residential properties, the firm's commissions include schools, offices, hotels, restaurants, retail, and furniture in the United States, Central America, and the Caribbean.

Amagansett Dunes
Amagansett, New York

This extraordinary house faces west toward the street, the afternoon sun, and prevailing winds. Its west and east facades contain operable glass, with small adjustable openings on the west side and large openings on the leeward east side, creating a pressure differential that promotes cooling cross breezes. The 1,725-square-foot (160-square-meter) house has an innovative full-height louver system made of canvas wrapped around a frame with tapered strips that increase their transparency on the southwest edge. The louvers create privacy from the street and cast dappled light patterns on the interior throughout the day. Viewed from the street at night, the facade looks like a woven lantern.

Promised Land
Amagansett, New York

This 4,135-square-foot (384-square-meter) stone, timber, and glass house is tuned to the wind, giving its owners cues to when conditions are optimal for water sports such as kite boarding and sailing. The house sprawls along an east-west axis, and a circulation bridge connects public spaces on one side with the private zone on the other, allowing prevailing winds to flow uninterrupted through the site. As the sun rotates around the house, its rays bounce off the surface of a parallel pool, projecting wind conditions via rippling light onto the ceilings of adjacent spaces. The structural system comprises a series of exposed glulam beams joined by steel flitch plates that create a void for light fixtures and cantilever to support the thin roof. They capture the wind, directing it along the beams like a wind tunnel. Aromatic lavender and mint are planted on the windward side so their scent is carried inside.

Robin's Way
Amagansett, New York

This 2,000-square-foot (186-square-meter) transformation of a 1960s kit house involved a gut renovation that preserved its post and beam construction. Natural rope was woven between the existing ceiling joists in a digitally fabricated framework of patterns that signify varying ceiling conditions, filter light, and hide speakers and utilities from view while baffling background noise. Dark stained cedar siding wraps the exterior and frames the new windows and doors. Interior walls were resurfaced in reclaimed barn wood, including behind a glass-lined shower, lending a feeling of showering outdoors. The design demonstrates how conventional materials can be used innovatively to marry old and new.

Sam's Creek
Bridgehampton, New York

Sam's Creek, in Bridgehampton, New York, consists of several open-ended boxes that focus the view from the street through the house to the landscape behind it. Mahogany boards wrap floors, ceilings, and walls to create the sense of an aperture and create privacy. Between the volumes, travertine terraces flow upward as siding on portions of the boxes, and the stone's proportion and repetition reference the area's wood shingle vernacular. Inside, the 6,500-square-foot (604-square-meter) home contains a variety of materials including timber, glass, and bronze.

CHARLES WRIGHT ARCHITECTS

Queensland, Australia

Charles Wright Architects (CWA) is an innovative design practice in idyllic Port Douglas, Far North Queensland. The business, founded in 2004, has a second office in Melbourne. Wright's training as a sculptor and painter is evident in the sculptural and compositional qualities of his buildings, which are often built on challenging sites.

The Edge
Queensland, Australia

This home in Port Douglas occupies a discreet plot beneath a popular public lookout and has far-reaching views of Four Mile Beach. Cantilevering it away from the hill resolved privacy issues while meeting view preservation requirements and affording the owners an uninterrupted views. The outdoor terrace is flanked by a concrete day bed on one side and a stunning infinity pool on the other side that runs around the perimeter of the house.

Re-Newell
Queensland, Australia

Re-Newell is a formidable dwelling in tropical North Queensland, though the original dwelling was modest and remains so from the street. The clients' original brief was to create a low-maintenance beach house suitable for the high-end holiday rental market. What makes the home so appealing is the large, open-plan living area with expansive views of the ocean. The neutral interior uses concrete, timber, and glass to their full potential, including floor-to-ceiling bi-fold doors that allow uninterrupted views of the Coral Sea.

Stamp House
Queensland, Australia

Stamp House sits on an environmentally senstive, off-grid site in Cape Tribulation, North Queensland. It was designed to offset the carbon it produces through systems such as water harvesting, solar energy generation, an on-site sewage treatment plant, and graywater recycling. Its shell is made from a combination of precast and poured-in-place concrete that can withstand the region's powerful cyclones.

Wright House
Queensland, Australia

Wright House, in the heart of Port Douglas, was engineered to withstand cyclones and mitigate the effects of the humid climate. It is elevated on piers to allow air to circulate underneath. The big "whale tail" roof—doubly insulated and separately ventilated— keeps the occupants cool while acting as a thermal chimney to pull air through the house, and shallow pools aid in evaporative cooling. Wood pergolas extend from the building, creating dappled light, and every room opens to the outdoors—the kitchen and living room through continuous bi-fold doors. Inside, joinery and ceilings are clear finished plywood.

CHARLES WRIGHT ARCHITECTS

GLR ARQUITECTOS

Garza García, Nuevo León, México

GLR Arquitectos is owned by Harvard University graduate Gilberto L. Rodríguez. He has been recognized in more than thirty states for his contribution to innovative building design, including both commercial projects and many contemporary residential homes. Gilberto is also a professor of projects at the Monterrey Institute of Technology and Higher Education.

Casa BC
Monterrey, Nuevo León, México

Casa BC is a 15,608-square-foot (1,450-square-meter) home in picturesque Monterrey, and its elevated position provides far-reaching views of the National Park of Chipinque. Its distinctive geometric cantilevered design lends a lightness to the heavy volumes defined by black granite, concrete, and exposed steel. Inside, the bedrooms, decks, home theater, and home office revolve around a double-height living room with dramatic skylights. Oriented to the sun's trajectory, the home is also a study in resource efficiency with water harvesting and graywater systems, solar water heaters, and native vegetation.

Casa CG

Monterrey, Nuevo León, México

Casa CG occupies a corner lot with glorious views of a park. Due to height restrictions, a basement area was excavated to meet the client's program requirements. The result is a three-level dwelling with three bedrooms and two spacious living areas. The interior materials are predominantly stone, timber, and glass.

Casa CH
Monterrey, Nuevo León, México

Casa CH, in Monterrey, is situated on a steep hill with unrivaled views of the city. The home's three levels offer the owners 9,687 square feet (1,900 square meters) of premium living space including five bedrooms, a six-car garage, home theater system, wine cellar, and gymnasium. Outdoor spaces feature a covered terrace, two bathrooms, and a swimming pool.

Casa Torres
Monterrey, Nuevo León, México

High in the Sierra Madre mountain range, Casa Torres seeks to connect with its natural environment. Visitors enter by crossing a reflecting pool built around a huge oak tree. Inside, the entry area features Santo Tomas marble and volcanic stone walls. The living room, essentially a glass box, offers a view of the Sierra Madre peaks and an outdoor garden with an inviting fireplace. The nearly 6,000-square-foot (552-square-meter) house also has a roof terrace, accessed via the dining room and the media room, offering spendid views of the mountains and the city of Monterrey.

JACKSON CLEMENTS BURROWS

Melbourne, Australia

JCB was established in 1998 by Tim Jackson, Jon Clements, and Graham Burrows. The office of fifty has completed a variety of project types, including in Asia and Europe.

Bangkok House
Bangkok

The two-story Bangkok House, in central Bangkok, has 7,534 square feet (700 square meters) of premium living space divided across two wings—one for the children and one for the parents. It's designed for the warm tropical environment with many outdoor areas and pools for relaxation and play.

Golden Crust Bakery
Melbourne, Australia

Golden Crust Bakery is an 8,611-square-foot (800-square-meter) home for a blended family with six children in Armadale, Melbourne. Originally an industiral warehouse, it had been unsympathetically renovated in a mock French provincial style. The clients asked JCB to restore the beautiful warehouses to their former integrity. One of the most striking features of the transformation is an architectural bridge that divides the main house from the former stables, which the teenage children occupy. Inside is a rich material palette of timber, stone, and glass.

JACKSON CLEMENTS BURROWS

Tree House
Melbourne, Australia

Tree House, on a steep, forested hillside on the fringe of Separation Creek, has views of the Wye River Peninsula and beyond. Its plan echoes the form of a tree with a central volume and rooms cantilevering in all directions. The upper-level core houses the dining room and kitchen, with projections for the entry and study, a sunroom to the west, a living area, and a cantilevered deck overlooking the ocean. A half-level down, the master bedroom wing lies just off the stair landing, projecting into the bush to the east. The lower level contains two bedrooms, a bath, and a laundry. Even though the residence is only 2,368 square feet (220 square meters), it makes a bold statement. Its exterior cement sheet panels, drawn from the local vernacular of 1950s fiber-cement-clad "fibro" beach shacks, are painted two tones of green to blend with the vegetation.

JACKSON CLEMENTS BURROWS

Trojan House
Melbourne, Australia

Trojan House is in the highly desirable suburb of Hawthorn. The clients asked JCB to design a playful, spacious addition for the growing family, which includes children under age ten. Successful elements of the design include a cantilevering container with kids' bedrooms and a bathroom upstairs and living spaces downstairs, and windows hidden behind perforated timber cladding. Interior circular windows scattered along the upstairs corridor and rooms establish visual connections between the two levels, while a thermal chimney enables conversation.

J. MAYER H. and PARTNERS

Berlin

J. MAYER H. and Partners was founded by Jürgen Mayer H. in 1996. In 2014, Andre Santer and Hans Schneider joined as partners. The company's main focus is to experiment with materials and technology. This has yielded some extraordinarily innovative designs, from single-family homes to commercial complexes.

Dupli Casa
Ludwigsburg, Germany

Dupli Casa was designed by Jürgen Mayer H., Georg Schmidthals, Thorsten Blatter, and Simon Takasaki. Its sculptural, futuristic white geometry is based on the footprint of an existing home built in 1984, and embodies the family history by "duplication and rotation." Its skin moves from outside to inside, where the material palette includes solid hardwood, marble, and glass.

JOH 3
Berlin

JOH 3 is a multi-family project with street-level commercial spaces in the popular district of Johannisstraße 3. The building offers a variety of living units ranging from townhouses with private gardens to luxurious penthouses, all of them outfitted with a range of highly designed materials. With its balconies, terraces, and planted interior courtyard, the sculptural, suspended facade draws on the notion of landscape in the city.

OLS House
Stuttgart, Germany

OLS House is a four-bedroom, three-story dwelling near Stuttgart with sensational views of the surrounding valley, and is situated alongside a range of conventional houses dating to the 1960s. Its interior centerpiece is a sculptural staircase, and floor-to-ceiling windows bathe the living areas in light. The elevated ground floor contains an entrance area, utility room, and spa; the second floor has an open-plan living room, dining room, and kitchen, while bedrooms, dressing areas, and bathrooms are upstairs.

Sonnenhof

Jena, Germany

Sonnenhof is a large-scale development comprising four new buildings with office and residences in historic Jena. The separate structures allow for through-ways on the grounds, and their placement at the edges of the plot created a small-scale outdoor space in the middle in keeping with the medieval city pattern. One of the futuristic-looking buildings has a central twisting, glazed staircase connecting several levels.

LAIDLAW SCHULTZ ARCHITECTS

Corona del Mar, California

Laidlaw Schultz Architects was founded in 1992 by Scott Laidlaw and Craig Schultz. The company employs a close-knit team of associates that works on both commercial and residential buildings. Notable commercial achievements include Cedars-Sinai Medical Center, Paramount Pictures, 20th Century Fox Studios, and Warner Bros. Studios.

Atomic Ranch
Corona del Mar, California

This major remodel of a midcentury modern home in Southern California was designed to accommodate the clients' expanding period furniture collection. The architects used large expanses of glass to capitalize on the modernist ideals of indoor-outdoor living and the panoramic Pacific Ocean views. Pocketing doors allow uninterrupted views and easy access to the terraces and pool.

LAIDLAW SCHULTZ ARCHITECTS

Cameo Highlands
Corona del Mar, California

Asked to design a home that fuses indoor and outdoor living, the architects created a series of courtyards and verandas that maximize views of the Pacific Ocean. The concept centers on two outdoor spaces. One is a walled entry courtyard with built-in seating, a fire pit, and raised planters. The second is a series of terraces on the lot's downhill slope that face the ocean. A quiet veranda overlooks the terraces where the owners garden. The house's cladding of smooth plaster and horizontal and vertical ipe planks adds material richness to the modern composition.

Harborview Hills
Corona del Mar, California

This California home's unassuming front facade opens to sensational coastal views. An interior courtyard contains sliding doors that turn the house into an outdoor pavilion facing the pool, where a scrim of foliage at the far end complements the sparkling blue water. Inside, aged wood flooring, lacquered cabinetry, marble kitchen countertops, and white-painted brick walls create a stylish backdrop to domestic life.

LAIDLAW SCHULTZ ARCHITECTS

LAIDLAW SCHULTZ ARCHITECTS

Stonehenge
Laguna Beach, California

Located near a busy intersection in a suburban hillside community, this house overcomes many challenges. The architects addressed the privacy issue with a series of peek-a-boo concrete pilasters that define a large entry courtyard. A naturalistic landscape on the street side mimics that of the steep site and valley beyond. Inside the courtyard, the sound of running water from a cleverly positioned fountain masks street sounds. Once inside, the house—a modern tree house— opens to a view of its hillside perch.

McBRIDE CHARLES RYAN

Victoria, Australia

McBride Charles Ryan is an award-winning architectural practice in Prahran, Victoria. At the helm are owner Debbie L. Ryan and director Robert McBride. With the assistance of a great supporting team of associates, they have grown the company exponentially. Projects range in scale from massive $200 million commercial buildings to innovative residential homes.

Cloud House
Melbourne, Australia

Cloud House is an ingenious, barrel-vaulted rear extension to a historic Edwardian residence in the Melbourne suburb of Fitzroy North. The red box houses a kitchen at the heart of the house and links the old and new structures. The cloud-like configuration is a dramatic space where family and friends congregate and where the lines between the floor and ceiling are playfully blurred.

McBRIDE CHARLES RYAN

Dome House
Melbourne, Australia

Dome House, in a conservative suburb of Melbourne, is a complex, curvaceous building centered around the idea of an eroded sphere that was buried and is rising from the earth. Parts of the sphere were selectively removed, leaving remnants that contain a garden shed, seat, letterbox, cellar, and meter enclosure, creating an intimate connection with the garden. While it is clearly modern, it has a composed, picturesque quality that resonates with the neighborhood sensibility.

Klein Bottle House
Victoria, Australia

Klein Bottle House is situated in idyllic Rye, on the Mornington Peninsula. Based on the complicated mathematical concept of the Klein Bottle, it passes the spiral back through itself in response to the difficult topography. Inside, a rectilinear platform and walls make the abstract geometry livable. A dramatic stair winds around an internal courtyard, passes the bedrooms as it ascends, and ends in the large living room, where hardwood, stone, and glass enhance the visual effect. The house is clad in cement sheeting, recalling folded origami and local fiber-cement-covered beach shacks.

McBRIDE CHARLES RYAN

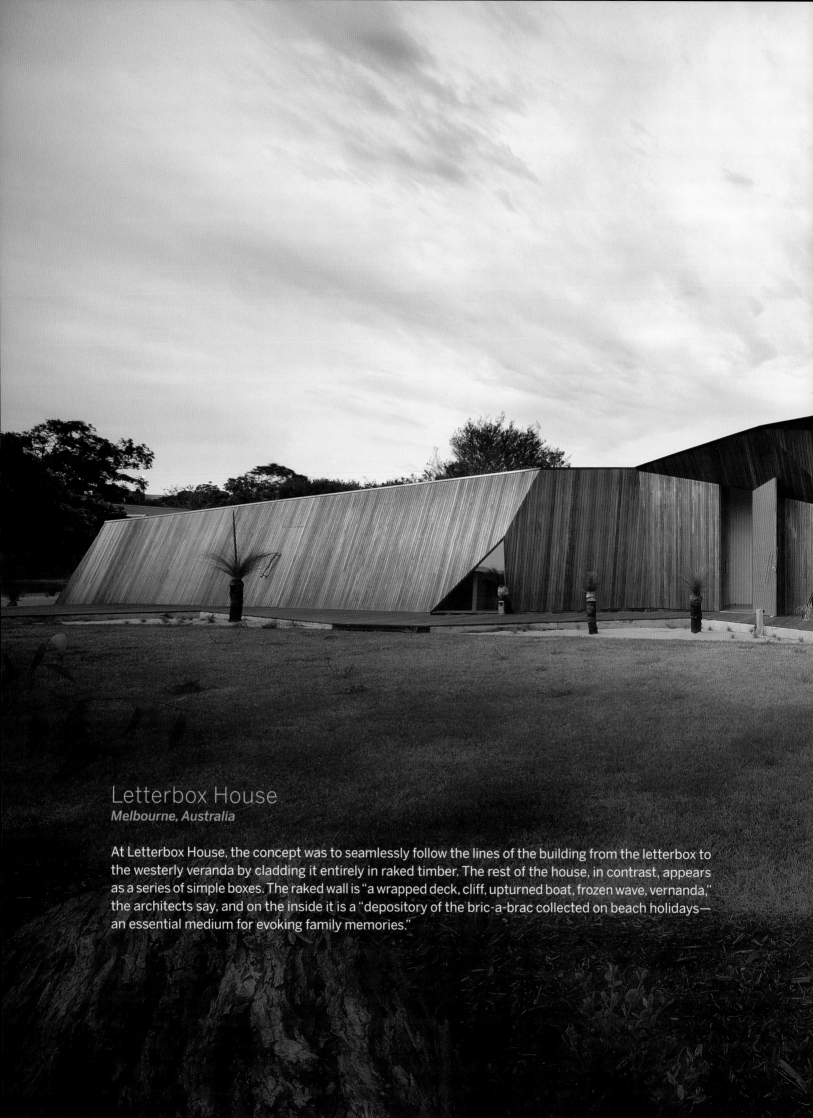

Letterbox House
Melbourne, Australia

At Letterbox House, the concept was to seamlessly follow the lines of the building from the letterbox to the westerly veranda by cladding it entirely in raked timber. The rest of the house, in contrast, appears as a series of simple boxes. The raked wall is "a wrapped deck, cliff, upturned boat, frozen wave, vernanda," the architects say, and on the inside it is a "depository of the bric-a-brac collected on beach holidays—an essential medium for evoking family memories."

McBRIDE CHARLES RYAN

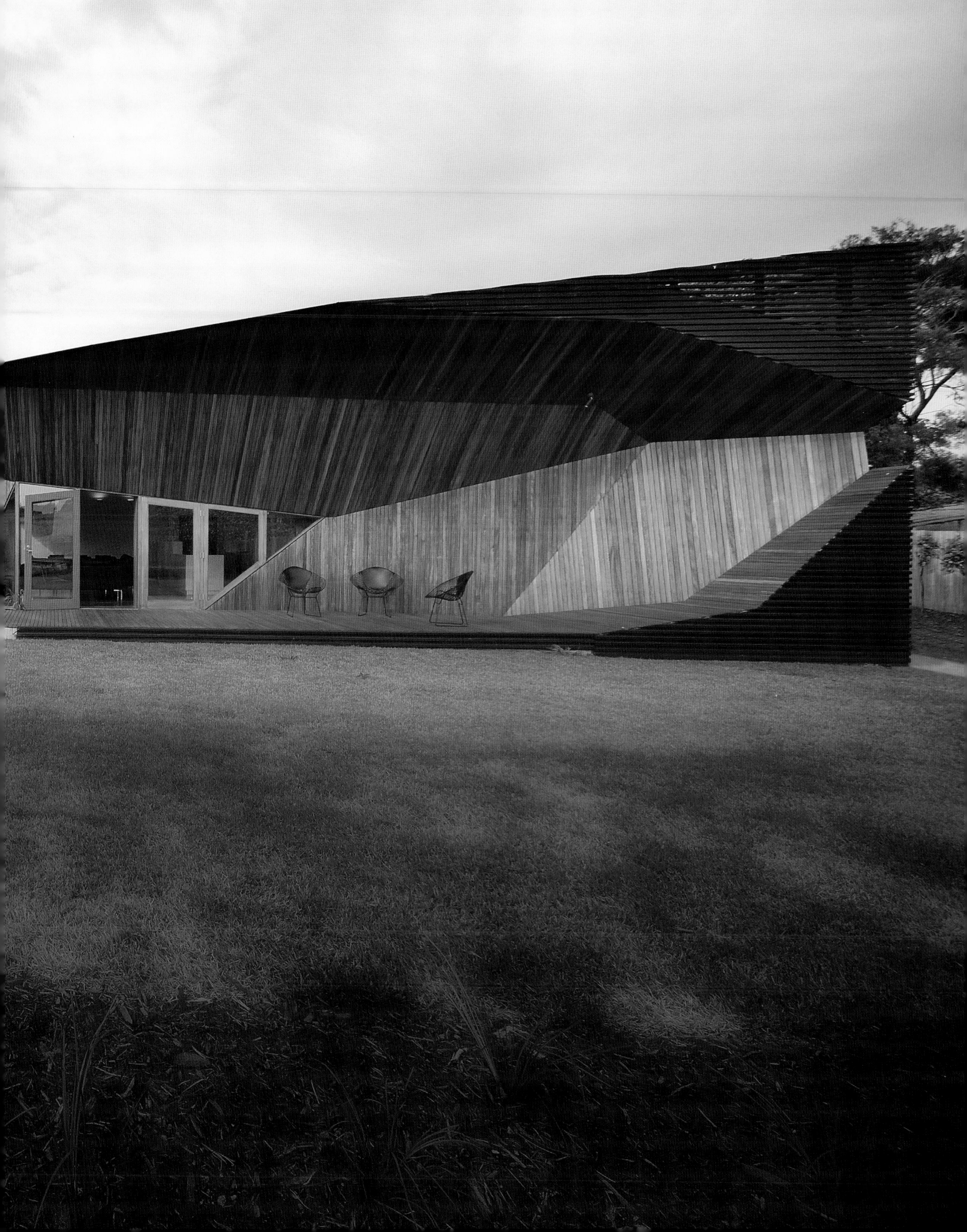

NICO VAN DER MEULEN ARCHITECTS

Johannesburg, South Africa

Nico van der Meulen is an innovative architectural practice founded in 1984 by Nico and his wife Santa. Over the last three decades, the business has grown substantially and now employs a team of top-notch architects and interior designers. The firm's primary focus is on cutting-edge design and functionality.

House Boz
Pretoria, South Africa

House Boz, in Mooikloof Heights, offers 8,310 square feet (772 square meters) of luxurious living space and was designed by Werner van der Meulen. Conceived as a "bush lodge" in its vast natural setting, the design features earthy square and rectangular rusted steel boxes and stone-clad walls that extend the house into the landscape.

Its abundant use of glass gives the dwelling a light and airy feel. The interior continues the use of natural materials with poured-in-place concrete, quartzite cladding, and rusted mild steel.

NICO VAN DER MEULEN ARCHITECTS

Kloof Road
Johannesburg, South Africa

Kloof Road sits at the foot of a nature reserve in Bedfordview, Johannesburg, and offers luxury on a grand scale at 11,840 square feet (1,100 square meters); every room opens to the outdoors. The double-height living room, dining room, and kitchen have a polished concrete floor that extends out to the lanai. Angled columns supporting steel beams and the roof pierce the soaring space and add a striking sculptural element. The house contains four en suite bedrooms, two children's bedroms, and a guest bedroom downstairs. Upstairs is the main bedroom suite, along with a lounge and playroom overlooking the living spaces. The lounge leads onto a large balcony that faces north toward the garden and distant views. Efficient operations were ensured with a radiant floor heating system powered by solar panels and a heat pump for both heating and cooling.

Sar
Johannesburg, South Africa

A dimly lit, pitched-roof house in Atholl was transformed with the use of expansive glass, concrete, and a framework of steel columns and beams. The raised, floating flat roof with a clerestory illuminates the living rooms, while a small atrium lets morning light into the kitchen and helps to cool the house at night. Louvered planes conceal four garages.

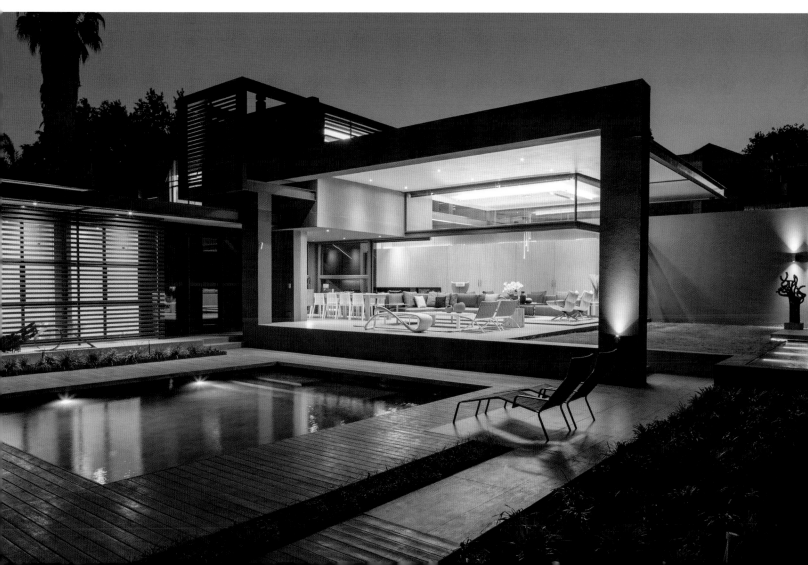

House The
Johannesburg, South Africa

House The, in Constantia Kloof, is a 2011 gut renovation that added a bedroom aerie, gym, roof deck, porte cochère, lanai, and infinity pool. The porte cochère roof is dramatically suspended from a semi-circular beam supported by the bisecting wall, a huge column, and a transfer beam. The architets raised the family room roof, creating a double-volume space with huge north-facing windows. Frameless sliding and folding doors allow the kitchen, dining, and family rooms to integrate seamlessly with the lanai, an ideal setup for entertaining. The house was literally topped off with a spectacular new master suite that takes in views to the north.

OFIST

Istanbul

Ofist is a progressive interior architecture practice in Tophane, Istanbul. The business, established in 2004, is the brainchild of Yasemin Arpac and Sabahattin Emir. The firm has designed innovative solutions for a range of discerning clients from private residential commissions to cafés, restaurants, bars, shops, and luxury hotels.

AD House
Istanbul

AD House is in a historic building in the bohemian area of Cihangir. Asked to modernize the 969-square-foot (90-square-meter) apartment in a way that enhances its former glory, Ofist embraced the exposed brick walls, polished timber flooring, decorative plaster moldings, and vaulted ceilings that give the property a rich character. Using a light touch, the architects installed a modular kitchen. In the bathroom they removed the impractical clawfoot tub, replacing it with a freestanding shower stall on wheels and fitting it with flexible hoses—a mobile setup that allows for easy cleaning. Rather than recreate the past, their approach was to design features that blend with the spirit of the place.

Bell House
Istanbul

Bell House is a large flat on the fourth floor of a historic building in Taksim called Hamit Bey, designed a century ago by renowned architect Apostol Mavrodoglu. The client approached Ofist to restore the residence faithfully to its original condition while adding modern luxuries. The property has an abundance of period character such as cast iron radiators, decorative plaster moldings, and timber flooring.

OFIST

Karakoy Loft
Istanbul

Karakoy Loft is an extravagant bachelor pad in the hub of Istanbul with delightful views of the Getronagan Armenian church and Galata Tower. Although the loft is only 1,938 square feet (180 square meters), Ofist maximized the space by enlarging windows and adding a mezzanine. The generous use of timber, iron, stone, and concrete lends a striking industrial appearance.

White House
Istanbul

White House is a luxurious penthouse in a forty-year-old extension of a historical building. The clients requested a light and spacious environment with large windows to maximize the city views. This involved completely reconfiguring the layout and inserting a custom spiral staircase with access to the roof garden. A marble bathroom, bespoke kitchen, and solid hardwood flooring add quiet drama and style.

OFIST

RANGR STUDIO

New York

Rangr Studio was founded by Yale graduate Jasmit Singh Rangr, an Indian-born architect who has worked for renowned firms such as Joseph Allen Stein and Gluckman Mayner Architects (now Gluckman Tang Architects). In addition to residential commissions, Rangr worked on the design of the Mori Arts Center in Tokyo and the Bronx Charter School.

RANGR STUDIO

Broadway Loft
New York

Broadway Loft has twenty-eight windows offering premium views across the rivers to New Jersey and Long Island. Flush door panels and clerestory glass help to pre-serve the view of the entire arched ceiling and all of the windows, thus creating the illusion of endless space. A steel and wood stair climbs to the roof, which has a hot tub, fireplace, and kitchen and lounge area. The staircase—a single strin-ger and pencil-thin steel rods that support the steps and handrail, forms a screen between the loft's public and private zones.

Cabin in the Woods
Southampton, New York

Cabin in the Woods is a woodland retreat with two master suites and three additional bedrooms—enough room for a family of five and their friends. The long cantilevered sections gaze out on the surrounding forest and carve out space beneath for a shaded patio and large infinity pool. A screened porch on one of the cantilevered ends contains a fireplace and creates the feeling of being in a treehouse. The wood-clad interior makes the house feel warm and inviting.

Casa Kimball
Cabrera, Dominican Republic

Casa Kimball, an exclusive rental villa in the Dominican Republic, has eight suites, each with a breathtaking view of the Pacific Ocean. Its 20,000 square feet (1,858 square meters) also include a dining room centered on the long infinity pool and two lounges. The garden areas incorporate two outdoor lounges, a bar, and a hot tub at cliff's edge.

House on Shookville Road
Milan, New York

This home was inspired by a transformed chicken coop that the clients had previously rented while on vacation in the area. The hillside residence appears modest from the street, but opens in the back to a deck and stone terrace with views of the Catskill Mountains. The architects used the foundation as a retaining wall, opening up the walk-out level with windows and doors. The new home contains four bedrooms, two and a half bathrooms, a large open-plan living/kitchen/dining area, and a family room.

SAOTA

Cape Town, South Africa

SAOTA is an international architectural firm whose members include Stefan Antoni, Philip Olmesdahl, Greg Truen, Phillippe Fouché, and Mark Bullivant, with support from a dedicated team of designers and technology and marketing experts. SAOTA has projects in the corporate, institutional, commercial, and residential marketplace. With roots in South Africa, the firm has an international footprint with projects on five continents.

Beachyhead
Plettenberg Bay, South Africa

Beachyhead is a 12,658-square-foot (1,176-square-meter) coastal home. The clients requested a relaxing environment that capitalizes on the water views and a place where they could entertain regularly with their many friends. Living spaces are suspended in a concrete box that floats over the site. Connected to a garden on the street side, the building overlooks a pool on the beach side and is clad in rough-textured concrete.

Clifton 2A
Clifton, South Africa

Clifton 2A is positioned on a challenging plot in a Cape Town suburb. Perched on the ridge below Lions Head, the house's design takes advantage of 270-degree views of the Atlantic Ocean, Camps Bay, and the Twelve Apostles beyond. Elemental materials such as stone, wood, and concrete lend an earthy feel to the interior, and long expanses of glass open the house to the stunning view.

OVD 919
Cape Town, South Africa

This 10,505-square-foot (976-square-meter) home on Bantry Bay capitalizes on the 360-degree mountain and sea views. Its concrete exterior is a contrast to the copper roof. Interior features include polished concrete flooring, solid oak joinery, floor-to-ceiling glazing, and a sculptural staircase.

Silver Bay
Shelley Point, South Africa

Shelley Point, on South Africa's West Coast, has glorious ocean vistas and is home to dolphins, whales, and migrating birds. The clients asked for a tranquil holiday home they could enjoy with family and friends. Its rustic contemporary appearance pays homage to traditional courtyard houses in the region. To achieve this effect, SAOTA used a variety of materials such as thatch, timber, granite, glass, and

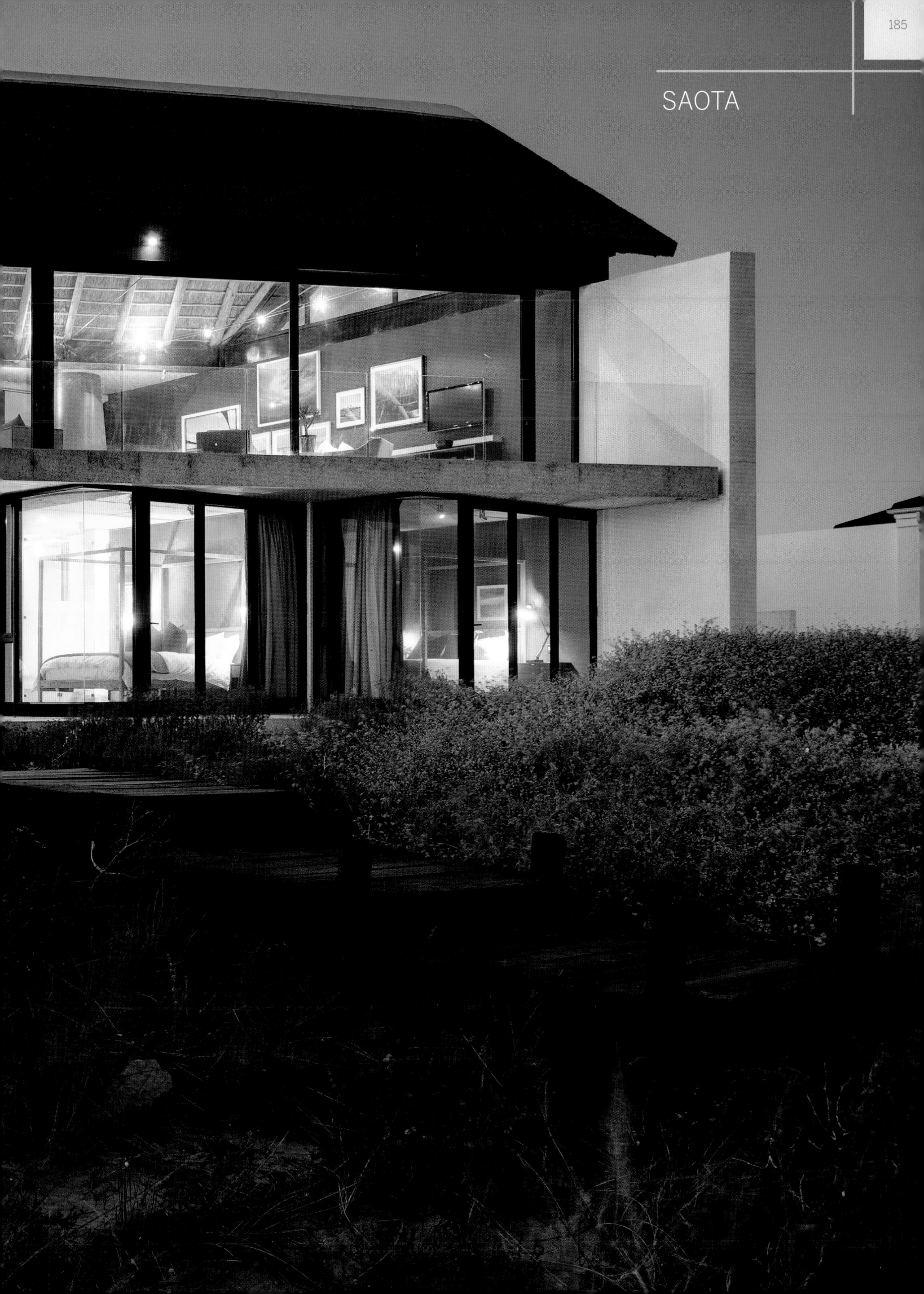

SAUNDERS
ARCHITECTURE

Bergen, Norway

Canadian-born architect Todd Saunders founded Saunders Architecture in 1998. The firm has worked on cultural and residential projects in Norway, England, Denmark, Italy, Sweden, and Canada.

Fogo Island Inn
Newfoundland, Canada

This five-star inn on Fogo Island was commissioned by the Shorefast Foundation, which requested a timeless piece of architecture that would boost economic activity on the island. The exterior of the twenty-nine-room property is mainly clad in wood and has large windows with breathtaking views of the sea. In addition to its luxury room accommodations, the inn has a restaurant, library, movie theater, art gallery, and spa facilities.

SAUNDERS ARCHITECTURE

Fogo Island, Squish Studio
Newfoundland, Canada

Located just outside the small town of Tilting on the eastern end of Fogo Island, Newfoundland, Squish Studio is one of six artist studios aimed at preserving the island's arts traditions. The studio is just 322 square feet (thirty square meters), but visually it punches well above its weight, thanks to its striking design and dramatic location high on the coastline.

Villa S
Bergen, Norway

Villa S measures 115 feet (35 meters) long and twenty feet (6 meters) wide; its elevated position creates the illusion that it is floating in the forest and provides a covered outdoor terrace beneath. The two volumes blend with the natural surroundings, thanks to the timber-clad exterior, huge windows, and open, cantilevered terrace.

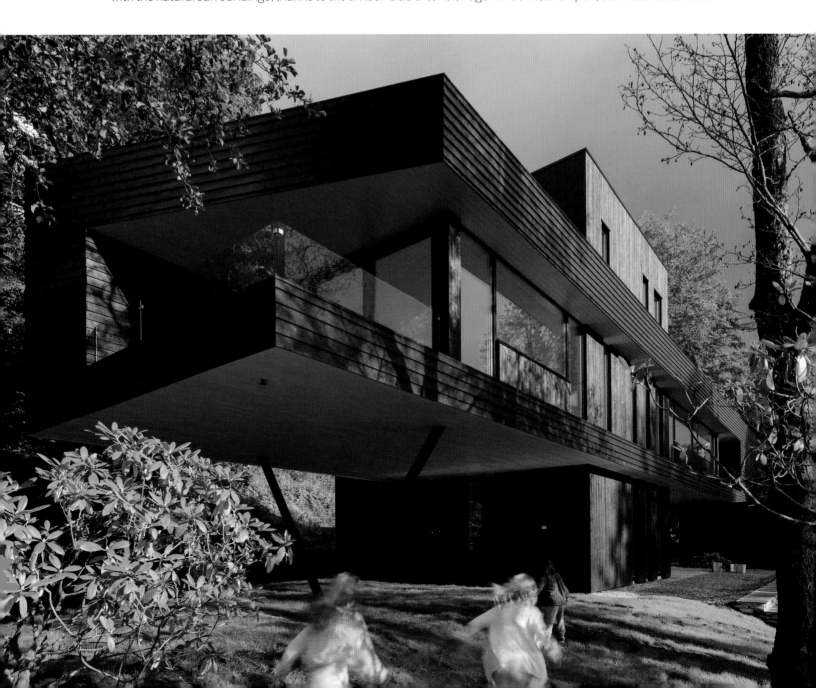

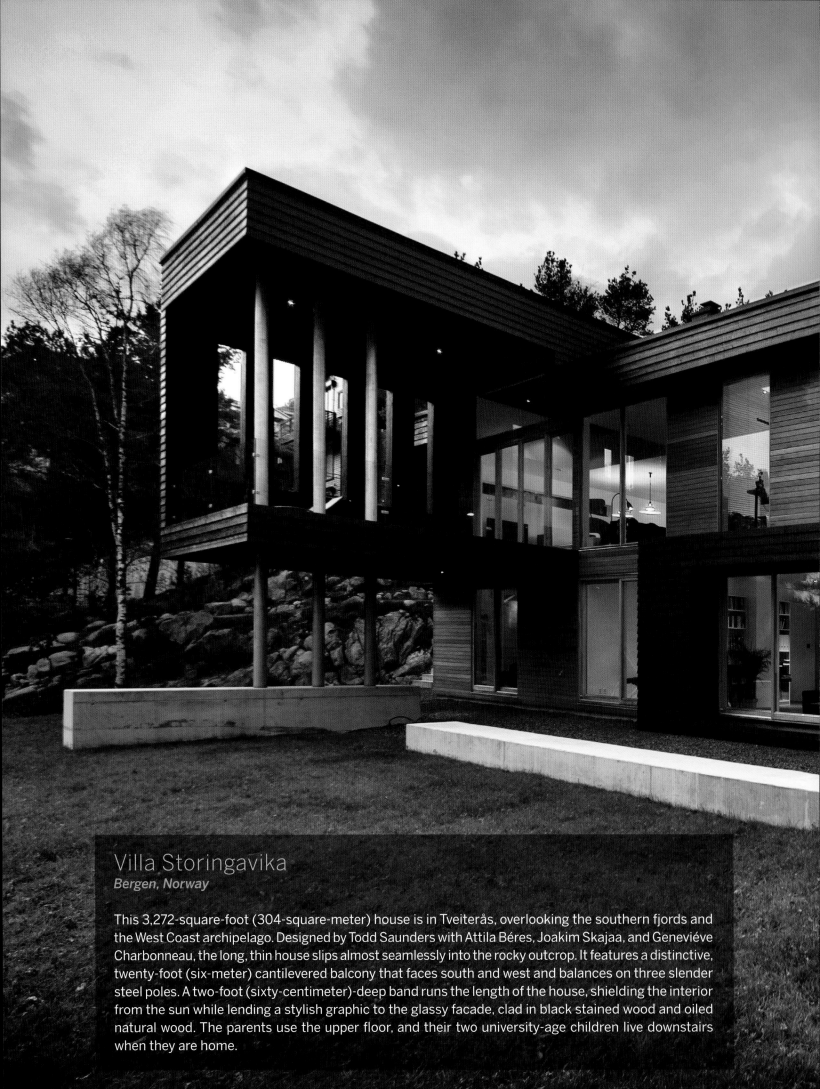

Villa Storingavika
Bergen, Norway

This 3,272-square-foot (304-square-meter) house is in Tveiterås, overlooking the southern fjords and the West Coast archipelago. Designed by Todd Saunders with Attila Béres, Joakim Skajaa, and Geneviéve Charbonneau, the long, thin house slips almost seamlessly into the rocky outcrop. It features a distinctive, twenty-foot (six-meter) cantilevered balcony that faces south and west and balances on three slender steel poles. A two-foot (sixty-centimeter)-deep band runs the length of the house, shielding the interior from the sun while lending a stylish graphic to the glassy facade, clad in black stained wood and oiled natural wood. The parents use the upper floor, and their two university-age children live downstairs when they are home.

SAUNDERS ARCHITECTURE

UNStudio

Amsterdam

UNStudio (United Network Studio) was founded by Ben van Berkel and Caroline Bos in 1988. In the last few years they expanded the business by opening offices in Shanghai and Hong Kong. In addition to residential work, the firm specializes in interior and product design, urban development, and infrastructure projects.

Haus am Weinberg
Stuttgart, Germany

Haus am Weinberg is in the heart of Stuttgart with envious views of a vineyard on one side and the cityscape on the other. Its unusual, futuristic appearance responds to the surrounding terraced landscape. At its heart is a curving, sculptural staircase that twists to direct circulation and brings in outside views. The light-filled interior is accentuated with solid oak flooring, natural stone, and white clay stucco walls speckled with small fragments of reflective stone.

UNStudio

Mobius House
Het Gooi, Netherlands

Mobius House, in picturesque Het Gooi, took five years to complete and consists of two interlocking lines. Its design concept is based on the mathematical Mobius band, represented by an intertwining loop that relates to the family's twenty-four-hour living and working cycle. The building skillfully incorporates concrete and glass to achieve a contemporary, minimalistic effect.

WIND House
North-Holland, Netherlands

In a small coastal village in North Holland, WIND House occupies a site between the woods and a polder landscape. Working and sleeping rooms occupy the back of the house, intimately enclosed by the woods, while glassy living areas in front enjoy views of the polder. The four facades curve to create petal-like wings that cross at the center of the house, where an open staircase connects the front and back wings. The exterior cladding highlights the home's sculptural form. A home automation system controls the electrical system, including solar panels.

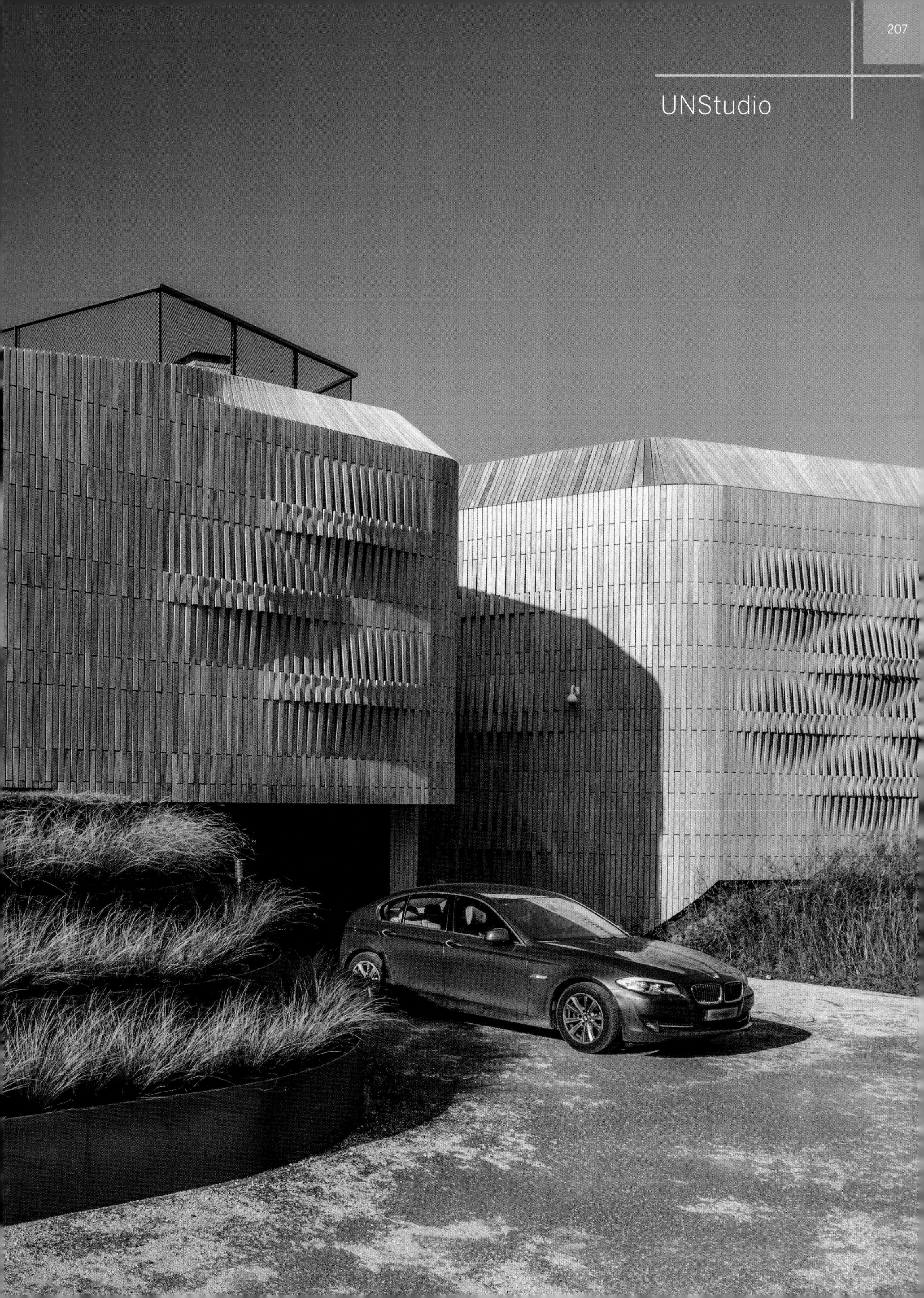

Villa NM
Upstate New York

This house in New York has a radical configuration that responds to its sloping site. One volume follows the northern slope; the other is elevated to create a covered parking space. The transition is accomplished structurally with five parallel walls that rotate along a horizontal axis from vertical to horizontal. Inside, the glassy, 3,229-square-foot (300-square-meter) house has a neutral, light-colored palette that puts the landscape front and center.

WHIPPLE RUSSELL ARCHITECTS

Los Angeles

Whipple Russell Architects, formerly known as Russell Group Architects, is managed by Marc Russell, the son of a diplomat, who spent much of his childhood overseas. This experience exposed him to many different styles of buildings. The company works on exclusive residential homes and large commercial projects.

Harold Way
Hollywood Hills, California

Harold Way, in Hollywood Hills's famed Bird Streets enclave, is modernist architecture at its finest. The client requested a contemporary dwelling that would also showcase his car. Floor to ceiling glass panels—along with pivoting, twelve-foot-high glass doors that open the kitchen to the deck—frame the shimmering city views. Other features include a state-of-the-art kitchen and a lounge/dining area featuring a modular dining table. When not in use, the table seating is pushed together to form a glossy cube.

Hopen Place
Hollywood Hills, California

Hopen Place, in Hollywood Hills's exclusive Bird Streets neighborhood, is a 4,800-square-foot (446-square-meter) remodel of a 1960s house. The interior features an organic palette of materials such as wood and stone, while expanses of glass offer uninterrupted city vistas. Water is integrated into the design with an infinity pool, reflecting pools, and a wet-edge waterfall along the walkway to the theater. A master bedroom was added to the footprint and floats out to the edge of the property, with a home theater tucked beneath.

WHIPPLE RUSSELL ARCHITECTS

Mandeville Canyon
Brentwood, California

The owners asked the architects to create a fusion of Italian architecture and New York loft. Marc Whipple designed a 7,000-square-foot (650-square-meter) modern ranch for the couple, both artists, with open, cleanly defined spaces that flow into one another. What makes this residence so distinctive are the thick, clay-colored walls with portals that create light patterns throughout the day. The wood floors, cleverly positioned windows, earthy colors, and sculptural concrete kitchen island lend a feeling that is both romantic and contemporary.

Walker Road
Great Falls, Virginia

This 6,700-square-foot (622-square-meter) house in a suburb of Washington, DC, takes full advantage of views of the surrounding treetops and distant valley. It is organized around a central walnut staircase that connects the main floor with the master suite above and the teenagers' bedrooms on the lower level. The exterior composition of glass and thin horizontal elements culminates in a large cantilevered terrace overlooking the view.

Photo Credits

CONCRETE HOUSE | *Luis H. Segovia*
HOUSE IN MADRID | *Santiago Cobreros*
LOS LAGOS | *Santiago Cobreros*
SV HOUSE | *Victor Sajara*

GLASS HOUSE | *Martin Gardner*
LIGHTHOUSE 65 | *Martin Gardner*
RICHMOND HOUSE | *Martin Gardner*
PILOT'S HOUSE | *Martin Gardner*

BREEZE | *Nacasa & Partners*
ROSIE | *Nacasa & Partners*
SHELL | *Nacasa & Partners*
SRK | *Nacasa & Partners*

COPPER HAUS | *Assemblage Studio/Drew Gregory*
HOUSE IN 2 PARTS | *Studio J Inc./Eric Jamison*
HOUSE OF LIGHT AND WATER | *Stephen Morgan Photography*
J2 RESIDENCE | *Bill Timmerman*

AMAGANSETT DUNES | *Bates Masi + Architects*
PROMISED LAND | *Bates Masi + Architects*
ROBIN'S WAY | *Bates Masi + Architects*
SAM'S CREEK | *Bates Masi + Architects*

THE EDGE | *Patrick Bingham-Hall*
RE-NEWELL | *Patrick Bingham-Hall*
STAMP HOUSE | *Patrick Bingham-Hall*
WRIGHT HOUSE | *Patrick Bingham-Hall*

CASA BC | *Jorge Taboada*
CASA CG | *Jorge Taboada*
CASA CH | *Jorge Taboada*
CASA TORRES | *Jorge Taboada*

BANGKOK HOUSE | *John Gollings*
GOLDEN CRUST BAKERY | *Shannon McGrath*
TREE HOUSE | *John Gollings*
TROJAN HOUSE | *Emma Cross, Gollings Photography*

DUPLI CASA | *David Franck*
JOH 3 | *Ludger Paffrath and Patricia Parinejad*
OLS HOUSE | *David Franck*
SONNENHOF | *David Franck*

ATOMIC RANCH | *John Ellis*
CAMEO HIGHLANDS | *John Ellis*
HARBORVIEW HILLS | *Larry Falke*
STONEHENGE | *John Ellis*

CLOUD HOUSE | *John Gollings*
DOME HOUSE | *John Gollings*
KLEIN BOTTLE HOUSE | *John Gollings*
LETTERBOX HOUSE | *John Gollings*

HOUSE BOZ | *David Ross and Barend Roberts*
KLOOF ROAD | *David Ross and Barend Roberts*
SAR | *David Ross and Barend Roberts*
HOUSE THE | *David Ross and Barend Roberts*

AD HOUSE | *Ali Bekman*
BELL HOUSE | *Ali Bekman*
KARAKOY LOFT | *Koray Erkaya*
WHITE HOUSE | *Ali Bekman*

BROADWAY LOFT | *Paul Warchol*
CABIN IN THE WOODS | *Paul Warchol*
CASA KIMBALL | *Paul Warchol*
HOUSE ON SHOOKVILLE ROAD | *Mikiko Kikuyama*

BEACHYHEAD | *Adam Letch*
CLIFTON 2A | *Adam Letch*
OVD 919 | *Adam Letch*
SILVER BAY | *Adam Letch*

FOGO ISLAND INN | *Bent René Syneevåg, Alex Fradkin, Iwan Baan*
FOGO ISLAND, SQUISH STUDIO | *Bent René Syneevåg*
VILLA S | *Bent René Syneevåg*
VILLA STORINGAVIKA | *Michael Putterman*

HAUS AM WEINBERG | *Iwan Baan and Christian Richters*
MOBIUS HOUSE | *Christian Richters*
WIND HOUSE | *Inga Powilleit (interior) and Fedde de Weert (exterior)*
VILLA NM | *Christian Richters*

HAROLD WAY | *Whipple Russell Architects*
HOPEN PLACE | *William MacCollum*
MANDEVILLE CANYON | *Cris Costea*
WALKER ROAD | *William MacCollum*